Growing Pains

By: Presh

Growing Pains

Copyright © 2025 By Precious Blackwell

All rights reserved. No part of this work may be used or reproduced, transmitted, stored, or used in any form or by any means graphic, electronic, or mechanical, including but not limited to photocopying, recording, scanning, digitizing, taping, Web distribution, information networks or information storage and retrieval systems, or in any manner whatsoever without prior written permission.

Printed in the United States of America.

ISBN-13: 979-8-218-59558-6 (Precious Blackwell)

Thank you for taking the time to read my work of art. You are appreciated. I hope that you enjoy this masterpiece.

Poems

STUCK	page 2
MASKING THE PAIN	page 3
BROKEN DOWN	page 4
THE TOUCH / QUALITY TIME	page 5
AFFIRMED	page 6
LOOKING BACK	page 7
REST IN PEACE	page 8
AMAZINGLY PHENOMENAL	page 9
POUND AFTER POUND	page 10
TO WHOM DOES A BLACK LIFE MATTER	page 11
LEAH'S STORY	page 12
DEEP / DIFFERENT / WHAT I WANTED VS WHAT I GOT	page 13
ALONE	page 14
HER PRAYER	page 15
EXPECTED EXPECTATIONS	page 16
STEPPIN OUT	page 17
LOST DREAMS	page 18
TRUTH IS	page 19
POSITIVE VIBES ONLY	page 20
LOVE DEFFERED	page 21
TIME	page 22
JUST US	page 23
WHAT YOU MEAN TO ME	page 24

THE GREAT FALL	page 25
BEING A BLACK WOMAN	page 26
IF TOMORROW NEVER COMES	page 27
DIM	page 28
IN MY ABSENCE	page 29
ARE YOU READY	page 30
IT'S COMPLICATED	page 31

STUCK

Drowning in a sea of defeat

Throwing pity parties in my head

Playing the blame game like it's not partly my fault

Short-term decisions with long-term consequences

Shifted my mission.

Visions of a better tomorrow

Halted

I'm still here

Stuck

MASKING THE PAIN

And through your eyes, I thought I would live another life

Away from the nightmares, the things that I've done, and the pain I've caused

Sick to my stomach as I write this

Some things are better left unsaid

Or are they?

Ran away from the struggle

Right into the arms of torment

The grass aint always greener on the other side

The pain nonetheless remains

BROKEN DOWN

The moment I feel everything is alright
One thing after another
My world starts to shatter around me
Like a recurring nightmare.
I try to tuck myself away from everyone
to escape
Escape from battling demons'
Masked as thoughts
I can't ignore
I'm breaking down mentally physically
and emotionally
I know I'm not alone
and although I appear strong
I need someone to check on me too.

THE TOUCH

I melted in her arms

The way she pulled me close

Sent chills up my spine

I exhaled

Clinging to that moment

QUALITY TIME

Time doesn't exist when I'm with you

It's just us in one space

Enjoying each others presence

Just being in the same room with you

Breathing the same air

Means the world to me

These are the moments

I crave

These are the memories I love to create

AFIRMED

When everything around me is falling apart

You're right there to remind me of who I am

And what I'm capable of

You breathe peace and reason

Into the illogic's around me

You pour into relishing and quenching my thirst for

Love and Life.

LOOKING BACK

I failed me, loving you
I didn't know it at the time
I loved you so deep and hard
I forgot about loving myself
I invested in love
I thought was reciprocal
I lacked boundaries
Self-love and Self-care.
My happiness joy, and pleasure
Revolved around you
I followed you for many seasons
Trying to rekindle a one-sided connection
Took some time for me to realize
The truth

REST IN PEACE

How do you wrap your head around

Waking up to never seeing a loved one again

All you have is memories

Days become weeks

Weeks become months

Month become Years

And that same pain resides deep down in your heart

It's inevitable

We all have an appointed time

That doesn't negate the fact

That losing someone hurts like hell

Deep down to your core

AMAZINGLY PHENOMENAL

Intrigued by the beauty in her eyes

She is a work of art

Masterfully crafted

God surely took his time

Beautifully flawed

She is the smile on my face

Butterflies in my stomach

The stars I gaze at, at night

She is amazingly phenomenal

POUND AFTER POUND

Eating my pain away

Pound after Pound

In the midst of my turmoil food is my safe space

I put my worries to the side

And devour a feast

Not missing a drop

Only to feel empty inside when I'm done

Pound after Pound

I'm killing myself slowly

Most of the time I can barely breathe

The worse off I am inwardly

The more I want to indulge

To release the pain

Even though it doesn't last

In those mere moments I am fine

Pound after Pound

TO WHOM DOES A BLACK LIFE MATTER

Black Woman

Black Man

Black Child

What's the cost of your life?

We out here screaming justice for our people

Way too often

New trauma on old wounds

I'm all cried out

What will it take for US to come together?

And the question still remains

To whom does a black life really matter?

LEAH'S STORY

Born into a nightmare
Created outta lust
Dysfunction runs through my veins
My bloodline sex, drugs, scams and scandals
My norm presides in
Shootouts, overdoses and molestation
Daddy locked up
Momma strung out
Grandma in her own world
My cousins touching me
Inappropriately
Granddaddy on his last leg
I tried to end it all once
Tired of the life that chose me
I'm struggling
Don't know how much more I can take
Hope someone reads this
Before it's too late.

DEEP

I'm on a cloud laying here next to you

I'm thinking about you like I'm missing you

Now that's DEEP

                                        DIFFERENT

                                  We are not the same

                                    We will never be

                                        I am who I am

                                      I can only be me

WHAT I WANTED VS WHAT I GOT

Friends forever

I thought we'd be

I never wanted you to be

A season

ALONE

Where did we go wrong

When did things get so bad

That distance

Feels better than spending time with one another

I love you

But I'd rather be alone

HER PRAYER

God

I come to you broken

In need of a fix

Begging for your blessings

Free me of my sins

I just want to go back to normalcy

Everything I was before

The backtracking

The backsliding

The drugs and abuse

I want to do right

Be better for myself

I've burned all my bridges

I have no one else

EXPECTED EXPECTATIONS

I expected you to love me
You broke my heart
I expected you to be there for me
You Weren't
I expected loyalty
And you deceived me
Further adding to this wall of mistrust
I had to learn the hard way
Everything isn't as expected

STEPPIN OUT

There's no way that I should be worried

When I trust that everything will be ok

My thoughts became clear visions

And my wildest dreams came true

The moment

I

Stepped out on FAITH

LOST DREAMS

I used to dream

But lately, I haven't been dreaming

Instead

My mind racing

Trying to figure out my next move

Like I can predict the future

Forget taking it a day at a time

I have to know what's next

DAMN

The uncertainty is stressing

Overthinking is taxing

My faith is tested

I question God and myself

Cause this reality got me all messed up

And all I want to do is dream

TRUTH IS

I allowed myself to get in way over my head
I let my ego and pride get in the way of asking for help
And now I'm drowning
Gasping for breath

POSITIVE VIBES ONLY

My light shines its brightest

When I feel aligned with my purpose

Lifted

My Vibration is at its peak

At Peace

It's all Love and Light

And

<u>P</u>ositive <u>V</u>ibes <u>O</u>nly

LOVE DEFERRED

Sometimes I feel like I failed you

I dedicated so much time sweat blood and tears

At one point you consumed my whole life

Would of

No one has come close to giving me the feeling

you gave

Never felt more Alive

I Think of you often

Excited when I see you

It's hard for me to be near you

Without feeling some type of way

So, I take up time

Forcing myself to do things to forget you

Only making things worse

Cause I know deep down inside I need you

I want you

TIME

I was so ready to be grown

Now as an adult I often find myself wishing I was a kid again

The concept of time seems like an illusion

Here today gone tomorrow

Before you know it's 2030

Life seemed to move in slow motion we were younger

Now it never seems like there's enough time in the day

What happened?

JUST US

I'm aroused admiring your remarkable anatomy

Enjoying refreshing intentional conversation

About different perspectives

Sharing our experiences

As I gaze into your beautiful brown eyes

Delighted and oblivious to anything going on

Outside what we are sharing in this point in time

WHAT YOU MEAN TO ME

I write for peace of mind

When there's no one to talk to

My pen talks to the paper

And although it doesn't respond

I feel relieved

A weight has been lifted

And I'm no longer losing my mind

Or beating myself up

I'm able to let go of what has been holding me back

You saved me

You kept me afloat

I've told you things

I've never whispered to another soul

And you've kept my secrets

THE GREAT FALL

Assets of influence

With hidden agendas

Deceivers

With ulterior motives

Sown into the fabric that draped their foundation

Greed and Power

Divided the family

Causing the undoing of everything that was built

BEING A BLACK WOMAN

WE are the most hated beings in the world

For simply being who WE are

Yet we have to be kind with our words

Calculated in how we express our emotions

Used, Abused, and Misled

All the while being of service to those who hate us

~smile~

Being a BLACK woman is hard

IF TOMORROW NEVER COMES

If tomorrow never comes
Did you make today your best day?
Did you live your life to the fullest?
If tomorrow never comes
Were you all that you could be?
Were you walking in your purpose?
If tomorrow never comes
Did you give your all each day
Are you prepared for what's next?
If tomorrow never comes
Today, would you say
You've done all that you set out to do?

DIM

I dimmed my own light

At the expense of

Allowing others to shine their brightest

I jeopardized my present and future

Because I thrived to see others at their best

Neglecting myself

What is it about me

That's not deserving?

IN MY ABSENCE

And when my time here is done
Don't cry because you miss me
I've done what I came here to do
Sing, Dance and Rejoice
In my absence
Hopefully, I am not forgotten
I'm sure we will see one another again

ARE YOU READY?

She will

Give you

Show you

And spread Love

Only if you're worthy

She will take you beyond boundaries

Pour into you everything you need to elevate

She is abundant

She is a dream come true

A virtue from God to you

Take care of her

IT'S COMPLICATED

Should we blur the lines?
Between friends and lovers
Overstep boundaries
When we both belong to others
Because you with me
Me with you
Is where WE belong
Sometimes we connect with someone
On a level deeper than the surface
Everything about them amazes us
Being with them is euphoric
Sometimes we connect with someone
On a level deeper than the surface
Was it a coincidence?
Or meant to be
Do I stay or Do I leave?
The complications of a complicated situations

www.ingramcontent.com/pod-product-compliance
Lightning Source LLC
Chambersburg PA
CBHW070752050426
42449CB00010B/2431